ACKNOWLEDGEMENTS

Many thanks to everyone that offered their thoughts during the creation of Milo's story. Most of all, I am deeply grateful to my wife Deborah, my daughters Alexa and Elizabeth and my son-in-law Josh for putting up with my constantly texted updates and questions! Their encouragement meant the world to me.

Milo is a special dog in many ways. Above all else, he is a cherished member of our family. We are fortunate to have him in our lives. Thanks to his breeder, Beverly Nelson of Hickory Hill Boston Terriers, who gave him the love and care that puppies need to thrive in the world of humans. Our family is also thankful for Milo's leader, Linc (2000-2014) who taught baby Milo, by his beautiful example, how to love, how to trust and how to feel safe and confident in a world where many inhabitants are larger.

Illustration: Steve Berk

*Cover photo credit: Raymond Sumner

My name is Milo. I am a Boston Terrier from Boston, Massachusetts. I live with my family near Faneuil Hall where Boston began a long time ago.

Photo credit: Steve Berk

Photo credit: Steve Berk

There are three things I really love to do. I love to be with my family. It's fun taking walks with my Mom and Dad and playing with my aunts' dogs, Quincy and Penny, when they visit us in Boston.

Photo credit: Elizabeth Berk
Quincy

Photo credit: Alexandra Berk
Penny

I love going to work with my Dad every day. We work with children. He is a "feelings Doctor" and I am a "therapy dog." Dad calls me Dr. Milo. When someone is unhappy or worried or angry, my Dad and I talk and play. I love to play fetch.

Photo credit: Steve Berk

Dad does the talking part and I do the playing part, but sometimes he plays too. I help make it easier for kids to talk about their feelings. I do tricks, or I just hang out and get belly rubs.

Photo credit: Steve Berk

It's okay if someone doesn't feel like talking or playing.

Photo credit: Steve Berk

I love dock diving. My Dad stands at the end of a dock which is like a long sidewalk. In front of it is a swimming pool.

Photo credit: Carney's K9 Swim Club

He holds a toy that can float high up in the air. I sit at the other end of the dock and wait for him to drop his arm and say, "go, go, go." I hear my Mom call out, "jump big Milo, jump big!"

Photo credit: Mark Agerholm

When I get close to the end of the dock, Dad throws the toy in the air. That's when I jump as high and far as I can.

Photo credit: Mark Agerholm

Photo credit: Mark Agerholm

When the toy lands on the water, I grab it in my mouth and swim back to the dock to do it again. Two times I have jumped over 16 feet! That's a BIG jump.

Photo credit: Mark Agerholm

Photo credit: Da-Rill Photography

When I jump at a dock diving event, a person called a "judge" writes down how far all the dogs have jumped. The dogs who jumped the longest get ribbons for first place, second place and third place. When my jumps are not as far as I hoped, Mom and Dad are still proud of me for trying my best

Photo credit: Steve Berk

Getting a ribbon is nice but I have fun just jumping into the water. Sometimes I get to wear a bathing suit with my name on it.

Photo credit: Unknown

Photo credit: Mark Agerholm

I jump at lots of different places. Mom and Dad call it "practice." Practice helps you get better at things. I call it FUN!

Photo credit: Brandon Fitts

Photo credit: Deborah Berk

Lots and lots of fun!

Photo credit: Steve Berk

Photo credit: Deborah Berk

There are not a lot of smaller dogs like me that are dock diving dogs. I am called a "lap dog" or "featherweight" because I am 12 inches tall. I must jump farther than almost all the big dogs to get a ribbon. Sometimes my Mom hears people say, "What's that little dog doing here?" When they see me jump, they change their minds. Then they cheer for me!

Photo credit: Thomas Muncy

Photo credit: Steve Berk

Why do people call me, "Little Big Dog?" A contest was held and the three dogs who jumped the farthest got to go to the National Championships. I was the only small dog in the group.

Photo credit: Mark Agerholm

After my last jump, the announcer said, "Ladies and gentlemen, little Milo just won first place and is going to the Nationals." When I swam back, one of the people in the crowd cheered and shouted, Little Big Dog. I like that name.

CONGRATULATIONS Steve & Milo!

I flew with Mom and Dad in a plane that was big because the Nationals were far away. Flying is a lot like dock diving.

Photo credit: Steve Berk

Where's the dock? I don't see it.

Photo credit: Steve Berk

At the Nationals I came in second place in the Featherweight Division. Everybody cheered a lot when I finished my last jump.

Photo credit: Sue Muncy

Dad, would you read that to me please?

Photo credit: Sue Muncy

I couldn't wait to get back home to tell my friends how much fun I had.

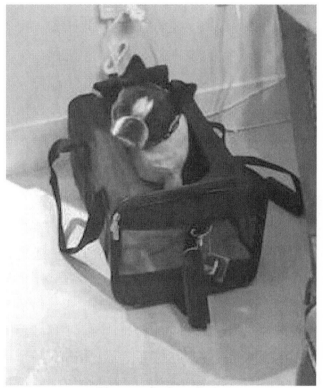

Photo credit: Steve Berk

Goodbye everybody. I hope I will be back next year.

Photo credit: Steve Berk

Here I am back at the office. I want you to know that it's not how big you are that counts, it's how big your heart is. Try your best and have fun!

Photo credit: Steve Berk

Maybe I`ll see you at the dock

Milo

"Mighty oaks from little acorns grow" -Chaucer,1374)

Photo credit: Public Domain

Illustration: Steve Berk

Made in the USA
Lexington, KY
03 June 2019